Personal PROMISES *from* GOD'S™ WORD

D0029462

WORLD PUBLISHING

Grand Rapids, Michigan 49418 U.S.A.

Copyright 1996 by World Publishing. All rights reserved.

The Scripture readings in this book have been taken from GOD'S WORD, copyright 1995 by God's Word to the Nations Bible Society. All rights reserved. Used by permission.

GOD'S WORD™ SERIES and its associated logo are trademarks of God's Word to the Nations Bible Society.

Up to 500 verses from *GOD'S WORD* may be quoted in any form (printed, written, visual, electronic, or audio) without written permission, provided that no more than half of any one book is quoted, and the verses quoted do not amount to more than 25% of the text of the work in which they are quoted. The designation (*GOD'S WORD*) must always appear after each quotation.

Developed and produced by The Livingstone Corporation. Project staff include: James C. Galvin, Christopher D. Hudson, Diane Krusemark, Mary Ann Lackland, and Brenda J. Todd.

Cover design by JMK Associates

ISBN 0529-10699-x

Library of Congress Catalog Card Number: 96-90384

Published by: World Publishing, Inc.
                  Grand Rapids, Michigan 49418 U.S.A.

Printed in the United States of America

1 2 3 4 5 6 7 8 00 99 98 97 96

❧ TABLE OF CONTENTS ❧

❦ INTRODUCTION ❧

Life can be painful. Throughout every year, friends fail us, family members disappoint us, and coworkers hurt us. Other frustrations, accidents, and sickness disrupt our lives. During these difficult times, we need reminders that God cherishes, loves, protects and cares for his children.

Personal Promises from GOD'S WORD was compiled to help you during these times. You'll find 100 topics that relate to the experiences and emotions that you may face each day. Each topic contains Scripture readings that relate to you and your situation.

Use this book of Bible promises for:

1) *Personal comfort:* When you need to feel God's warm care.

2) *Personal devotions:* When you want to apply God's word to your life.

3) *Personal or group study:* When you want to learn more about God, or teach a Bible study or Sunday school lesson.

All the readings come from the easy-to-read Bible translation, *GOD'S WORD*™. In many verses you will notice half-brackets (⌊ ⌋) in the text. These words were supplied by the translation team when the context contains meaning that is not explicitly stated in the original language.

We pray that *Personal Promises from GOD'S WORD* will lead you to discover the richness of God's word and of his promises to you.

 ANGER

The LORD is merciful, compassionate, patient,
and always ready to forgive.

Psalm 145:8

Be angry without sinning. Don't go to bed angry. Don't give the devil any
opportunity ⌊to work⌋.

Ephesians 4:26-27

Get rid of your bitterness, hot tempers, anger, loud quarreling, cursing,
and hatred. Be kind to each other, sympathetic, forgiving each other as
God has forgiven you through Christ.

Ephesians 4:31-32

Remember this, my dear brothers and sisters: Everyone should be quick to
listen, slow to speak, and should not get angry easily. An angry person
doesn't do what God approves of.

James 1:19-20

❧ **ANXIETY** ❧

Turn your burdens over to the LORD,
   and he will take care of you.
      He will never let the righteous person stumble.

Psalm 55:22

Trust the LORD with all your heart,
   and do not rely on your own understanding.
In all your ways acknowledge him,
   and he will make your paths smooth.

Proverbs 3:5-6

Don't be afraid, because I am with you.
Don't be intimidated; I am your God.
   I will strengthen you.
   I will help you.
   I will support you with my victorious right hand.

Isaiah 41:10

Never worry about anything. But in every situation let God know what you need in prayers and requests while giving thanks. Then God's peace, which goes beyond anything we can imagine, will guard your thoughts and emotions through Christ Jesus.

Philippians 4:6-7

Turn all your anxiety over to God because he cares for you.

1 Peter 5:7

∽ ASSURANCE ∽

Let go⌊of your concerns⌋!
>Then you will know that I am God.
>>I rule the nations.
>>I rule the earth.

Psalm 46:10

That's why I tell you to have faith that you have already received whatever you pray for, and it will be yours.

Mark 11:24

My sheep respond to my voice, and I know who they are. They follow me, and I give them eternal life. They will never be lost, and no one will tear them away from me. My Father, who gave them to me, is greater than everyone else, and no one can tear them away from my Father.

John 10:27-29

I am convinced that nothing can ever separate us from God's love which Christ Jesus our Lord shows us. We can't be separated by death or life, by angels or rulers, by anything in the present or anything in the future, by forces or powers in the world above or in the world below, or by anything else in creation.

Romans 8:38-39

I'm convinced that God, who began this good work in you, will carry it through to completion on the day of Christ Jesus.

Philippians 1:6

BELIEF

That's why I tell you to have faith that you have already received whatever you pray for, and it will be yours.

Mark 11:24

However, he gave the right to become God's children to everyone who believed in him.

John 1:12

God loved the world this way: He gave his only Son so that everyone who believes in him will not die but will have eternal life.

John 3:16

Whoever believes in the Son has eternal life, but whoever rejects the Son will not see life. Instead, he will see God's constant anger.

John 3:36

No one can please God without faith. Whoever goes to God must believe that God exists and that he rewards those who seek him.

Hebrews 11:6

❧ **BEREAVEMENT** ❧

Precious in the sight of the LORD
is the death of his faithful ones.

Psalm 116:15

Blessed are those who mourn.
They will be comforted.

Matthew 5:4

Don't be troubled. Believe in God, and believe in me. My Father's house has many rooms. If that were not true, would I have told you that I'm going to prepare a place for you? If I go to prepare a place for you, I will come again. Then I will bring you into my presence so that you will be where I am.

John 14:1-3

Brothers and sisters, we don't want you to be ignorant about those who have died. We don't want you to grieve like other people who have no hope. We believe that Jesus died and came back to life. We also believe that, through Jesus, God will bring back those who have died. They will come back with Jesus.

1 Thessalonians 4:13-14

He will wipe every tear from their eyes. There won't be any more death. There won't be any grief, crying, or pain, because the first things have disappeared.

Revelation 21:4

❦ BITTERNESS ❦

So if you are offering your gift at the altar and remember there that another believer has something against you, leave your gift at the altar. First go away and make peace with that person. Then come back and offer your gift.

Matthew 5:23-24

Love is patient. Love is kind. Love isn't jealous. It doesn't sing its own praises. It isn't arrogant. It isn't rude. It doesn't think about itself. It isn't irritable. It doesn't keep track of wrongs. It isn't happy when injustice is done, but it is happy with the truth.

1 Corinthians 13:4-6

Get rid of your bitterness, hot tempers, anger, loud quarreling, cursing, and hatred. Be kind to each other, sympathetic, forgiving each other as God has forgiven you through Christ.

Ephesians 4:31-32

Put up with each other, and forgive each other if anyone has a complaint. Forgive as the Lord forgave you.

Colossians 3:13

Try to live peacefully with everyone, and try to live holy lives, because if you don't, you will not see the Lord. Make sure that everyone has kindness from God so that bitterness doesn't take root and grow up to cause trouble that corrupts many of you.

Hebrews 12:14-15

❧ BLESSING ❧

I will make you a great nation,
I will bless you.
I will make your name great,
   and you will be a blessing.

Genesis 12:2

Today I'm giving you the choice of a blessing or a curse. You'll be blessed if you obey the commands of the LORD your God that I'm giving you today.

Deuteronomy 11:26-27

Blessed is the person who trusts the LORD.
The LORD will be his confidence.

Jeremiah 17:7

Praise the God and Father of our Lord Jesus Christ! Through Christ, God has blessed us with every spiritual blessing that heaven has to offer.

Ephesians 1:3

❧ BOLDNESS ❧

Wait with hope for the LORD.
Be strong, and let your heart be courageous.
Yes, wait with hope for the LORD.

Psalm 27:14

The LORD will be your confidence.
He will keep your foot from getting caught.

Proverbs 3:26

Don't be afraid, because I am with you.
Don't be intimidated; I am your God.

I will strengthen you.
I will help you.
I will support you with my victorious right hand.

Isaiah 41:10

You won't ⌊succeed⌋ by might or by power, but by my Spirit, says the LORD of Armies.

Zechariah 4:6b

I eagerly expect and hope that I will have nothing to be ashamed of. I will speak very boldly and honor Christ in my body, now as always, whether I live or die.

Philippians 1:20

I can do everything through Christ who strengthens me.

Philippians 4:13

So we can go confidently to the throne of God's kindness to receive mercy and find kindness, which will help us at the right time.

Hebrews 4:16

So we can confidently say,
   "The Lord is my helper.
      I will not be afraid.
         What can mortals do to me?"

Hebrews 13:6

❧ BRAVERY ❧

Don't be afraid of them, because the LORD your God is with you. He is a
great and awe-inspiring God.

Deuteronomy 7:21

You won't fight this battle. ⌊Instead,⌋ take your position, stand still, and see
the victory of the LORD for you, Judah and Jerusalem. Don't be frightened
or terrified. Tomorrow go out to face them. The LORD is with you.

2 Chronicles 20:17

With you I can attack a line of soldiers.
With my God I can break through barricades.

Psalm 18:29

The LORD is my strength and my shield.
My heart trusted him, so I received help.
My heart is triumphant; I give thanks to him with my song.

Psalm 28:7

Finally, receive your power from the Lord and from his mighty strength. . . .
For this reason, take up all the armor that God supplies. Then you will be
able to take a stand during these evil days. Once you have overcome all
obstacles, you will be able to stand your ground.

Ephesians 6:10, 13

Dear children, you belong to God. So you have won the victory over these people, because the one who is in you is greater than the one who is in the world.

1 John 4:4

∽ CARE OF GOD ∽

What is a mortal that you remember him
   or the Son of Man that you take care of him?

Psalm 8:4

He is our God
   and we are the people in his care,
      the flock that he leads.

Psalm 95:7a

O LORD, you have examined me, and you know me.
   You alone know when I sit down and when I get up.
   You read my thoughts from far away. . . .
   You are all around me—in front of me and in back of me.
   You lay your hand on me.

Psalm 139:1-2, 5

How precious are your thoughts concerning me, O God!
How vast in number they are!

If I try to count them,
> there would be more of them than there are grains of sand.
>> When I wake up, I am still with you.

Psalm 139:17-18

Don't ever worry and say, "What are we going to eat?" or "What are we going to drink?" or "What are we going to wear?" Everyone is concerned about these things, and your heavenly Father certainly knows you need all of them. But first, be concerned about his kingdom and what has his approval. Then all these things will be provided for you.

Matthew 6:31-33

Turn all your anxiety over to God because he cares for you.

1 Peter 5:7

⊱ CATASTROPHE ⊰

During times of trouble I called on the LORD.
> The LORD answered me ⌊and⌋ set me free ⌊from all of them⌋.
The LORD is on my side.
> I am not afraid.
>> What can mortals do to me?

Psalm 118:5-6

When you go through the sea, I am with you.
When you go through rivers, they will not sweep you away.
When you walk through fire, you will not be burned,
    and the flames will not harm you.

Isaiah 43:2

The LORD is good.
    ⌊He is⌋ a fortress in the day of trouble.
    He knows those who seek shelter in him.

Nahum 1:7

We know that all things work together for the good of those who love
God—those whom he has called according to his plan.

Romans 8:28

Praise the God and Father of our Lord Jesus Christ! He is the Father who
is compassionate and the God who gives comfort. He comforts us
whenever we suffer. That is why whenever other people suffer, we are able
to comfort them by using the same comfort we have received from God.

2 Corinthians 1:3-4

In every way we're troubled, but we aren't crushed by our troubles. We're
frustrated, but we don't give up. We're persecuted, but we're not
abandoned. We're captured, but we're not killed.

2 Corinthians 4:8-9

Never worry about anything. But in every situation let God know what you need in prayers and requests while giving thanks. Then God's peace, which goes beyond anything we can imagine, will guard your thoughts and emotions through Christ Jesus.

Philippians 4:6-7

CHANGE

I am convinced that nothing can ever separate us from God's love which Christ Jesus our Lord shows us. We can't be separated by death or life, by angels or rulers, by anything in the present or anything in the future, by forces or powers in the world above or in the world below, or by anything else in creation.

Romans 8:38-39

Don't become like the people of this world. Instead, change the way you think. Then you will always be able to determine what God really wants—what is good, pleasing, and perfect.

Romans 12:2

Whoever is a believer in Christ is a new creation. The old way of living has disappeared. A new way of living has come into existence.

2 Corinthians 5:17

Jesus Christ is the same yesterday, today, and forever.

Hebrews 13:8

❧ COMFORT ❧

Even though I walk through the dark valley of death,
   because you are with me, I fear no harm.
      Your rod and your staff give me courage.

Psalm 23:4

But from everlasting to everlasting,
   the LORD's mercy is on those who fear him.
      His righteousness belongs
         to their children and grandchildren.

Psalm 103:17

This is my comfort in my misery:
   Your promise gave me a new life.

Psalm 119:50

Let your mercy comfort me
   as you promised.

Psalm 119:76

Come to me, all who are tired from carrying heavy loads, and I will give you rest.

Matthew 11:28

I'm leaving you peace. I'm giving you my peace. I don't give you the kind of peace that the world gives. So don't be troubled or cowardly.

John 14:27

Praise the God and Father of our Lord Jesus Christ! He is the Father who is compassionate and the God who gives comfort. He comforts us whenever we suffer. That is why whenever other people suffer, we are able to comfort them by using the same comfort we have received from God.

2 Corinthians 1:3-4

∼ COMPLAINTS ∼

Do everything without complaining or arguing. Then you will be blameless and innocent. You will be God's children without any faults among people who are crooked and corrupt. You will shine like stars among them in the world.

Philippians 2:14-15

I'm not saying this because I'm in any need. I've learned to be content in whatever situation I'm in. I know how to live in poverty or prosperity. No matter what the situation, I've learned the secret of how to live when I'm full or when I'm hungry, when I have too much or when I have too little. I can do everything through Christ who strengthens me.

Philippians 4:11-13

Welcome each other as guests without complaining.

1 Peter 4:9

❦ CONFIDENCE ❧

The LORD is my light and my salvation.
    Who is there to fear?
The LORD is my life's fortress.
    Who is there to be afraid of?

Psalm 27:1

It is better to depend on the LORD
    than to trust mortals.

Psalm 118:8

You won't ⌊succeed⌋ by might or by power, but by my Spirit, says the LORD of Armies.

Zechariah 4:6b

But he told me: "My kindness is all you need. My power is strongest when you are weak." So I will brag even more about my weaknesses in order that Christ's power will live in me.

2 Corinthians 12:9

So we can confidently say,
  "The Lord is my helper.
   I will not be afraid.
      What can mortals do to me?"

Hebrews 13:6

✎ CONTENTMENT ✎

Naked I came from my mother,
  and naked I will return.
The LORD has given,
  and the LORD has taken away!
May the name of the LORD be praised.

Job 1:21

Be happy with the LORD,
  and he will give you the desires of your heart.

Psalm 37:4

I'm not saying this because I'm in any need. I've learned to be content in whatever situation I'm in. I know how to live in poverty or prosperity. No matter what the situation, I've learned the secret of how to live when I'm full or when I'm hungry, when I have too much or when I have too little. I can do everything through Christ who strengthens me.

Philippians 4:11-13

Don't love money. Be happy with what you have because God has said, "I will never abandon you or leave you."

Hebrews 13:5

God's divine power has given us everything we need for life and for godliness. This power was given to us through knowledge of the one who called us by his own glory and integrity.

2 Peter 1:3

∾ **COURAGE** ∾

I have commanded you, "Be strong and courageous! Don't tremble or be terrified, because the LORD your God is with you wherever you go."

Joshua 1:9

The LORD is my light and my salvation.
    Who is there to fear?

The LORD is my life's fortress.
    Who is there to be afraid of?

Psalm 27:1

Wait with hope for the LORD.
Be strong, and let your heart be courageous.
Yes, wait with hope for the LORD.

Psalm 27:14

He gives strength to those who grow tired
    and increases the strength of those who are weak.

Isaiah 40:29

"Don't be afraid of people. I am with you, and I will rescue you," declares
the LORD.

Jeremiah 1:8

But he told me: "My kindness is all you need. My power is strongest when
you are weak." So I will brag even more about my weaknesses in order that
Christ's power will live in me. Therefore, I accept weakness, mistreatment,
hardship, persecution, and difficulties suffered for Christ. It's clear that
when I'm weak, I'm strong.

2 Corinthians 12:9-10

CRISIS

He pulled me out of a horrible pit,
    out of the mud and clay.
He set my feet on a rock
    and made my steps secure.

Psalm 40:2

God is our refuge and strength,
    an ever-present help in times of trouble.

Psalm 46:1

We know that all things work together for the good of those who love
God—those whom he has called according to his plan.

Romans 8:28

Praise the God and Father of our Lord Jesus Christ! He is the Father who
is compassionate and the God who gives comfort. He comforts us
whenever we suffer. That is why whenever other people suffer, we are able
to comfort them by using the same comfort we have received from God.

2 Corinthians 1:3-4

❧ **DANGER** ❧

The LORD's beloved people will live securely with him.
   The LORD will shelter them all day long.

Deuteronomy 33:12b

I fall asleep in peace the moment I lie down
   because you alone, O LORD, enable me to live securely.

Psalm 4:8

He hides me in his shelter when there is trouble.
He keeps me hidden in his tent.
He sets me high on a rock.

Psalm 27:5

You have been my refuge,
   a tower of strength against the enemy.
I would like to be a guest in your tent forever
   and to take refuge under the protection of your wings.

Psalm 61:3-4

Whoever lives under the shelter of the Most High
   will remain in the shadow of the Almighty.

I will say to the LORD,
"⌈You are⌉ my refuge and my fortress, my God in whom I trust."

Psalm 91:1-2

You have been a refuge for the poor,
a refuge for the needy in their distress,
a shelter from the rain, and shade from the heat.

Isaiah 25:4a

⛬ **DEATH** ⛬

Even though I walk through the dark valley of death,
because you are with me, I fear no harm.
Your rod and your staff give me courage.

Psalm 23:4

Blessed are those who mourn.
They will be comforted.

Matthew 5:4

My Father's house has many rooms. If that were not true, would I have told you that I'm going to prepare a place for you? If I go to prepare a place for you, I will come again. Then I will bring you into my presence so that you will be where I am.

John 14:2-3

The reward for sin is death, but the gift that God freely gives is everlasting life found in Christ Jesus our Lord.

Romans 6:23

I am convinced that nothing can ever separate us from God's love which Christ Jesus our Lord shows us. We can't be separated by death or life, by angels or rulers, by anything in the present or anything in the future, by forces or powers in the world above or in the world below, or by anything else in creation.

Romans 8:38-39

So we are always confident. We know that as long as we are living in these bodies, we are living away from the Lord. Indeed, our lives are guided by faith, not by sight. We are confident and prefer to live away from this body and to live with the Lord.

2 Corinthians 5:6-8

This is the testimony: God has given us eternal life, and this life is found in his Son.

1 John 5:11

⚜ DECISIONS ⚜

A person's steps are directed by the LORD,
   and the LORD delights in his way.

Psalm 37:23

Trust the LORD with all your heart,
   and do not rely on your own understanding.
In all your ways acknowledge him,
   and he will make your paths smooth.

Proverbs 3:5-6

A person may plan his own journey,
   but the LORD directs his steps.

Proverbs 16:9

I know the plans that I have for you, declares the LORD. They are plans for peace and not disaster, plans to give you a future filled with hope.

Jeremiah 29:11

⚜ DEPRESSION ⚜

He is the healer of the brokenhearted.
He is the one who bandages their wounds.

Psalm 147:3

Yet, the strength of those who wait with hope in the LORD
will be renewed.
They will soar on wings like eagles.
They will run and won't become weary.
They will walk and won't grow tired.

Isaiah 40:31

He certainly has taken upon himself our suffering
and carried our sorrows,
but we thought that God had wounded him,
beat him, and punished him.
He was wounded for our rebellious acts.
He was crushed for our sins.
He was punished so that we could have peace,
and we received healing from his wounds.

Isaiah 53:4-5

Be humbled by God's power so that when the right time comes he will
honor you.
Turn all your anxiety over to God because he cares for you.

1 Peter 5:6-7

❦ **DEVOTION** ❦

I am the LORD your God, who brought you out of slavery in Egypt.
Never have any other god.

Exodus 20:2-3

Love the LORD your God with all your heart, with all your soul, and with all
your strength.

Deuteronomy 6:5

But if you don't want to serve the LORD, then choose today whom you will
serve. . . . My family and I will still serve the LORD.

Joshua 24:15

No one can serve two masters. He will hate the first master and love the
second, or he will be devoted to the first and despise the second. You
cannot serve God and wealth.

Matthew 6:24

Be devoted to each other like a loving family. Excel in showing respect for
each other. Don't be lazy in showing your devotion. Use your energy to
serve the Lord. Be happy in your confidence, be patient in trouble, and
pray continually.

Romans 12:10-12

∂∂ **DISAPPOINTMENT** ∂∂

Wait with hope for the LORD.
Be strong, and let your heart be courageous.
Yes, wait with hope for the LORD.

Psalm 27:14

The LORD is near to everyone who prays to him,
   to every faithful person who prays to him.

Psalm 145:18

"The mountains may move, and the hills may shake,
   but my kindness will never depart from you.
     My promise of peace will never change,"
      says the LORD, who has compassion on you.

Isaiah 54:10

But that's not all. We also brag when we are suffering. We know that
suffering creates endurance, endurance creates character, and character
creates confidence. We're not ashamed to have this confidence, because
God's love has been poured into our hearts by the Holy Spirit, who has
been given to us.

Romans 5:3-5

We know that all things work together for the good of those who love God—those whom he has called according to his plan.

Romans 8:28

∽ DISCOURAGEMENT ∽

Be strong, all who wait with hope for the LORD,
   and let your heart be courageous.

Psalm 31:24

Why are you discouraged, my soul?
Why are you so restless?
   Put your hope in God,
      because I will still praise him.
         He is my savior and my God.

Psalm 43:5

When I called, you answered me.
   You made me bold by strengthening my soul.

Psalm 138:3

I know the plans that I have for you, declares the LORD. They are plans for peace and not disaster, plans to give you a future filled with hope.

Jeremiah 29:11

At the same time the Spirit also helps us in our weakness, because we don't know how to pray for what we need. But the Spirit intercedes along with our groans that cannot be expressed in words. The one who searches our hearts knows what the Spirit has in mind. The Spirit intercedes for God's people the way God wants him to.

Romans 8:26-27

God is fair. He won't forget what you've done or the love you've shown for him.

Hebrews 6:10a

⊱ **DOUBTS** ⊰

Jesus said to Thomas, "You believe because you've seen me. Blessed are those who haven't seen me but believe."

John 20:29

Faith assures us of things we expect and convinces us of the existence of things we cannot see.

Hebrews 11:1

If any of you needs wisdom to know what you should do, you should ask God, and he will give it to you. God is generous to everyone and doesn't find fault with them. When you ask for something, don't have any doubts. A person who has doubts is like a wave that is blown by the wind and tossed by the sea. A person who has doubts shouldn't expect to receive anything from the Lord. A person who has doubts is thinking about two different things at the same time and can't make up his mind about anything.

James 1:5-8

∽ **ETERNAL LIFE** ∽

God loved the world this way: He gave his only Son so that everyone who believes in him will not die but will have eternal life.

John 3:16

I can guarantee this truth: Those who listen to what I say and believe in the one who sent me will have eternal life. They won't be judged because they have already passed from death to life.

John 5:24

My sheep respond to my voice, and I know who they are. They follow me, and I give them eternal life. They will never be lost, and no one will tear them away from me.

John 10:27-28

The reward for sin is death, but the gift that God freely gives is everlasting life found in Christ Jesus our Lord.

Romans 6:23

I'm telling you a mystery. Not all of us will die, but we will all be changed. It will happen in an instant, in a split second at the sound of the last trumpet. Indeed, that trumpet will sound, and then the dead will come back to life. They will be changed so that they can live forever.

1 Corinthians 15:51-52

This is the testimony: God has given us eternal life, and this life is found in his Son.

1 John 5:11

 FAITH

He told them, "Because you have so little faith. I can guarantee this truth: If your faith is the size of a mustard seed, you can say to this mountain, 'Move from here to there,' and it will move. Nothing will be impossible for you."

Matthew 17:20b

That's why I tell you to have faith that you have already received whatever you pray for, and it will be yours.

Mark 11:24

Now that we have God's approval because of faith, we have peace with God because of what our Lord Jesus Christ has done.

Romans 5:1

God saved you through faith as an act of kindness. You had nothing to do with it. Being saved is a gift from God.

Ephesians 2:8

Faith assures us of things we expect and convinces us of the existence of things we cannot see.

Hebrews 11:1

When you ask for something, don't have any doubts. A person who has doubts is like a wave that is blown by the wind and tossed by the sea.

James 1:6

∞ **FAITHFULNESS OF GOD** ∞

But you, O Lord, are a compassionate and merciful God.
You are patient, always faithful and ready to forgive.

Psalm 86:15

The LORD is good.
His mercy endures forever.
His faithfulness endures throughout every generation.

Psalm 100:5

What if some of them were unfaithful? Can their unfaithfulness cancel God's faithfulness? That would be unthinkable! God is honest, and everyone else is a liar.

Romans 3:3-4a

⮞ FAMILY ⮜

But if you don't want to serve the LORD, then choose today whom you will serve. . . . My family and I will still serve the LORD.

Joshua 24:15

Train a child in the way he should go,
    and even when he is old he will not turn away from it.

Proverbs 22:6

Who can find a wife with a strong character?
She is worth far more than jewels. . . .
Her children and her husband
    stand up and bless her.
In addition, he sings her praises.

Proverbs 31:10, 28

Children, obey your parents because you are Christians. This is the right thing to do. . . .

Fathers, don't make your children bitter about life. Instead, bring them up in Christian discipline and instruction.

Ephesians 6:1, 4

❧ FATHERHOOD OF GOD ❧

The God who is in his holy dwelling place
   is the father of the fatherless and the defender of widows.

Psalm 68:5

Even though you're evil, you know how to give good gifts to your children. So how much more will your Father in heaven give good things to those who ask him?

Matthew 7:11

However, he gave the right to become God's children to everyone who believed in him.

John 1:12

You are all God's children by believing in Christ Jesus.

Galatians 3:26

Because you are God's children, God has sent the Spirit of his Son into us to call out, "Abba! Father!" So you are no longer slaves but God's children. Since you are God's children, God has also made you heirs.

Galatians 4:6-7

Consider this: The Father has given us his love. He loves us so much that we are actually called God's dear children. And that's what we are. For this reason the world doesn't recognize us, and it didn't recognize him either.

1 John 3:1

∾ **FEAR** ∾

The LORD is my light and my salvation.
   Who is there to fear?
The LORD is my life's fortress.
   Who is there to be afraid of?

Psalm 27:1

I trust God.
I am not afraid.
   What can mortals do to me?

Psalm 56:11

He will put his angels in charge of you
   to protect you in all your ways.

Psalm 91:11

Don't be afraid, because I am with you.
Don't be intimidated; I am your God.
   I will strengthen you.

I will help you.
I will support you with my victorious right hand.

Isaiah 41:10

I'm leaving you peace. I'm giving you my peace. I don't give you the kind of peace that the world gives. So don't be troubled or cowardly.

John 14:27

You haven't received the spirit of slaves that leads you into fear again. Instead, you have received the spirit of God's adopted children by which we call out, "Abba! Father!"

Romans 8:15

God didn't give us a cowardly spirit but a spirit of power, love, and good judgment.

2 Timothy 1:7

∞ FORGIVENESS ∞

Purify me from sin with hyssop, and I will be clean.
Wash me, and I will be whiter than snow.
Let me hear ⌊sounds of⌋ joy and gladness.
Let the bones that you have broken dance.

Hide your face from my sins,
   and wipe out all that I have done wrong.

Psalm 51:7-9

As high as the heavens are above the earth—
   that is how vast his mercy is toward those who fear him.
As far as the east is from the west—
   that is how far he has removed our rebellious acts from himself.

Psalm 103:11-12

So those who are believers in Christ Jesus can no longer be condemned.

Romans 8:1

Put up with each other, and forgive each other if anyone has a complaint.
Forgive as the Lord forgave you.

Colossians 3:13

God is faithful and reliable. If we confess our sins, he forgives them and
cleanses us from everything we've done wrong.

1 John 1:9

∼ FRIENDSHIP ∼

Whoever forgives an offense seeks love,
  but whoever keeps bringing up the issue
    separates the closest of friends.

Proverbs 17:9

A friend always loves,
  and a brother is born to share trouble.

Proverbs 17:17

Friends can destroy one another,
  but a loving friend can stick closer than family.

Proverbs 18:24

Wounds made by a friend are intended to help,
  but an enemy's kisses are too much to bear.

Proverbs 27:6

∼ FUTURE ∼

If only they would fear me and obey all my commandments as long as they
live! Then things would go well for them and their children forever.

Deuteronomy 5:29

I know the plans that I have for you, declares the LORD. They are plans for peace and not disaster, plans to give you a future filled with hope.

Jeremiah 29:11

So don't ever worry about tomorrow. After all, tomorrow will worry about itself. Each day has enough trouble of its own.

Matthew 6:34

Therefore, be alert, because you don't know on what day your Lord will return.

Matthew 24:42

But as Scripture says:
   "No eye has seen,
      no ear has heard,
         and no mind has imagined
            the things that God has prepared
               for those who love him."

1 Corinthians 2:9

I'm telling you a mystery. Not all of us will die, but we will all be changed. It will happen in an instant, in a split second at the sound of the last trumpet. Indeed, that trumpet will sound, and then the dead will come back to life. They will be changed so that they can live forever.

1 Corinthians 15:51-52

∽ GOD'S WILL ∽

⌊The LORD says,⌋
   "I will instruct you.
   I will teach you the way that you should go.
   I will advise you as my eyes watch over you."

Psalm 32:8

A person's steps are directed by the LORD,
   and the LORD delights in his way.

Psalm 37:23

Trust the LORD with all your heart,
   and do not rely on your own understanding.
In all your ways acknowledge him,
   and he will make your paths smooth.

Proverbs 3:5-6

Entrust your efforts to the LORD,
   and your plans will succeed.

Proverbs 16:3

You mortals, the LORD has told you what is good.
   This is what the LORD requires from you:
      to do what is right,

to love mercy,
  and to live humbly with your God.

Micah 6:8

It is God who produces in you the desires and actions that please him.
Philippians 2:13

❧ GOODNESS OF GOD ❧

The LORD is good and decent.
  That is why he teaches sinners the way they should live.

Psalm 25:8

Taste and see that the LORD is good.
  Blessed is the person who takes refuge in him.

Psalm 34:8

God is truly good to Israel,
  to those whose lives are pure.

Psalm 73:1

You, O Lord, are good and forgiving,
  full of mercy toward everyone who calls out to you.

Psalm 86:5

The LORD is good to everyone
   and has compassion for everything that he has made.

Psalm 145:9

The LORD is good.
   ⌊He is⌋ a fortress in the day of trouble.
   He knows those who seek shelter in him.

Nahum 1:7

∽ GRIEF ∽

Blessed are those who mourn.
   They will be comforted.

Matthew 5:4

Come to me, all who are tired from carrying heavy loads, and I will give
you rest.

Matthew 11:28

I'm leaving you peace. I'm giving you my peace. I don't give you the kind of
peace that the world gives. So don't be troubled or cowardly.

John 14:27

At the same time the Spirit also helps us in our weakness, because we don't know how to pray for what we need. But the Spirit intercedes along with our groans that cannot be expressed in words.

Romans 8:26

We know that all things work together for the good of those who love God—those whom he has called according to his plan.

Romans 8:28

Praise the God and Father of our Lord Jesus Christ! He is the Father who is compassionate and the God who gives comfort. He comforts us whenever we suffer. That is why whenever other people suffer, we are able to comfort them by using the same comfort we have received from God.

2 Corinthians 1:3-4

Dear friends, don't be surprised by the fiery troubles that are coming in order to test you. Don't feel as though something strange is happening to you, but be happy as you share Christ's sufferings. Then you will also be full of joy when he appears again in his glory.

1 Peter 4:12-13

He will wipe every tear from their eyes. There won't be any more death. There won't be any grief, crying, or pain, because the first things have disappeared.

Revelation 21:4

∞ **GUIDANCE** ∞

Make your ways known to me, O LORD,
   and teach me your paths.
Lead me in your truth and teach me
   because you are God, my savior.
     I wait all day long for you.

Psalm 25:4-5

⌊The LORD says,⌋
   "I will instruct you.
   I will teach you the way that you should go.
   I will advise you as my eyes watch over you."

Psalm 32:8

Your word is a lamp for my feet
   and a light for my path.

Psalm 119:105

Trust the LORD with all your heart,
   and do not rely on your own understanding.
In all your ways acknowledge him,
   and he will make your paths smooth.

Proverbs 3:5-6

A nation will fall when there is no direction,
    but with many advisers there is victory.

Proverbs 11:14

Entrust your efforts to the LORD,
    and your plans will succeed.

Proverbs 16:3

A person may plan his own journey,
    but the LORD directs his steps.

Proverbs 16:9

It is God who produces in you the desires and actions that please him.
Philippians 2:13

If any of you needs wisdom to know what you should do, you should ask
God, and he will give it to you. God is generous to everyone and doesn't
find fault with them.

James 1:5

✎ GUILT ✎

I made my sins known to you, and I did not cover up my guilt.
I decided to confess them to you, O LORD.
    Then you forgave all my sins.

Psalm 32:5

Wash me thoroughly from my guilt,
   and cleanse me from my sin. . . .
Purify me from sin with hyssop, and I will be clean.
Wash me, and I will be whiter than snow.

Psalm 51:2, 7

   The sacrifice pleasing to God is a broken spirit.
   O God, you do not despise a broken and sorrowful heart.

Psalm 51:17

As high as the heavens are above the earth—
   that is how vast his mercy is toward those who fear him.
As far as the east is from the west—
   that is how far he has removed our rebellious acts from himself.

Psalm 103:11-12

Whoever covers over his sins does not prosper.
Whoever confesses and abandons them receives compassion.

Proverbs 28:13

He was wounded for our rebellious acts.
He was crushed for our sins.
   He was punished so that we could have peace,
      and we received healing from his wounds.
We have all strayed like sheep.

Each one of us has turned to go his own way,
  and the LORD has laid all our sins on him.

Isaiah 53:5-6

Because all people have sinned, they have fallen short of God's glory. They receive God's approval freely by an act of his kindness through the price Christ Jesus paid to set us free ⌊from sin⌋.

Romans 3:23-24

So those who are believers in Christ Jesus can no longer be condemned.

Romans 8:1

God is faithful and reliable. If we confess our sins, he forgives them and cleanses us from everything we've done wrong.

1 John 1:9

❦ HEALING ❦

Praise the LORD, my soul,
  and never forget all the good he has done:
He is the one who forgives all your sins,
  the one who heals all your diseases.

Psalm 103:2-3

He was wounded for our rebellious acts.
  He was crushed for our sins.

He was punished so that we could have peace,
    and we received healing from his wounds.

Isaiah 53:5

Heal me, O LORD, and I will be healed.
    Rescue me, and I will be rescued.
        You are the one I praise.

Jeremiah 17:14

That is why we are not discouraged. Though outwardly we are wearing out, inwardly we are renewed day by day.

2 Corinthians 4:16

If you are sick, call for the church leaders. Have them pray for you and anoint you with olive oil in the name of the Lord. (Prayers offered in faith will save those who are sick, and the Lord will cure them.) If you have sinned, you will be forgiven. So admit your sins to each other, and pray for each other so that you will be healed.

Prayers offered by those who have God's approval are effective.

James 5:14-16

❦ **HEAVEN** ❧

I heard every creature in heaven, on earth, under the earth, and on the sea. Every creature in those places was singing,

"To the one who sits on the throne and to the lamb
　be praise, honor, glory, and power forever and ever."

Revelation 5:13

He will wipe every tear from their eyes. There won't be any more death.
There won't be any grief, crying, or pain, because the first things have
disappeared.

Revelation 21:4

Nothing unclean, no one who does anything detestable, and no liars will
ever enter it. Only those whose names are written in the lamb's Book of
Life will enter it.

Revelation 21:27

❧ HELP OF GOD ☙

The LORD is my rock and my fortress and my Savior,
　my God, my rock in whom I take refuge,
　　my shield, and the strength of my salvation,
　　　my stronghold.

Psalm 18:2

You are my hiding place.
You protect me from trouble.
You surround me with joyous songs of salvation.

Psalm 32:7

We wait for the LORD.
   He is our help and our shield.

Psalm 33:20

God is our refuge and strength,
   an ever-present help in times of trouble.

Psalm 46:1

I look up toward the mountains.
   Where can I find help?
My help comes from the LORD,
   the maker of heaven and earth.

Psalm 121:1-2

The LORD is good.
   ⌊He is⌋ a fortress in the day of trouble.
   He knows those who seek shelter in him.

Nahum 1:7

However, the helper, the Holy Spirit, whom the Father will send in my name, will teach you everything. He will remind you of everything that I have ever told you.

John 14:26

At the same time the Spirit also helps us in our weakness, because we don't know how to pray for what we need. But the Spirit intercedes along with our groans that cannot be expressed in words.

Romans 8:26

HOPE

Why are you discouraged, my soul?
Why are you so restless?
Put your hope in God,
because I will still praise him.
He is my savior and my God.

Psalm 42:11

You are my hope, O Almighty LORD.
You have been my confidence ever since I was young.

Psalm 71:5

We were saved with this hope in mind. If we hope for something we already see, it's not really hope. Who hopes for what can be seen? But if we hope for what we don't see, we eagerly wait for it with perseverance.

Romans 8:24-25

May God, the source of hope, fill you with joy and peace through your faith in him. Then you will overflow with hope by the power of the Holy Spirit.

Romans 15:13

Faith assures us of things we expect and convinces us of the existence of things we cannot see.

Hebrews 11:1

✖ **HURTS** ✖

The LORD is near to those whose hearts are humble.
He saves those whose spirits are crushed.

Psalm 34:18

He is the healer of the brokenhearted.
He is the one who bandages their wounds.

Psalm 147:3

Blessed are you when people insult you,
   persecute you,
      lie, and say all kinds of evil things about you because of me.

Rejoice and be glad because you have a great reward in heaven!
　　The prophets who lived before you were persecuted in these ways.

Matthew 5:11-12

Come to me, all who are tired from carrying heavy loads, and I will give
you rest.

Matthew 11:28

❧ INSECURITY ☙

Those who know your name trust you, O LORD,
　　because you have never deserted those who seek your help.

Psalm 9:10

The LORD will be your confidence.
He will keep your foot from getting caught.

Proverbs 3:26

In the fear of the LORD there is strong confidence,
　　and his children will have a place of refuge.

Proverbs 14:26

What can we say about all of this? If God is for us, who can be against us?

Romans 8:31

The one who loves us gives us an overwhelming victory in all these difficulties.

Romans 8:37

I can do everything through Christ who strengthens me.

Philippians 4:13

So we can confidently say,
  "The Lord is my helper.
    I will not be afraid.
      What can mortals do to me?"

Hebrews 13:6

≈ INTIMIDATION ≈

The LORD is my light and my salvation.
  Who is there to fear?
The LORD is my life's fortress.
  Who is there to be afraid of?

Psalm 27:1

God is our refuge and strength,
  an ever-present help in times of trouble.
That is why we are not afraid

even when the earth quakes
or the mountains topple into the depths of the sea.

Psalm 46:1-2

His heart is steady, and he is not afraid.
In the end he will look triumphantly at his enemies.

Psalm 112:8

A person's fear sets a trap ⌊for him⌋,
but one who trusts the LORD is safe.

Proverbs 29:25

I, Jeremiah, said, "Almighty LORD, I do not know how to speak. I am only
a boy!"
   But the LORD said to me, "Don't say that you are only a boy. You will go
wherever I send you. You will say whatever I command you to say. Don't
be afraid of people. I am with you, and I will rescue you," declares the LORD.

Jeremiah 1:6-8

Be alert. Be firm in the Christian faith. Be courageous and strong.

1 Corinthians 16:13

Also pray that God will give me the right words to say. Then I will speak
boldly when I reveal the mystery of the Good News.

Ephesians 6:19

Don't let anyone look down on you for being young. Instead, make your speech, behavior, love, faith, and purity an example for other believers.

1 Timothy 4:12

∽ JEALOUSY ∽

Never desire to take your neighbor's wife away from him.
Never long for your neighbor's household, his field, his male or female slave, his ox, his donkey, or anything else that belongs to him.

Deuteronomy 5:21

Certainly, anger kills a stubborn fool,
   and jealousy murders a gullible person.

Job 5:2

Do not be preoccupied with evildoers.
Do not envy those who do wicked things

Psalm 37:1

A tranquil heart makes for a healthy body,
   but jealousy is ⌊like⌋ bone cancer.

Proverbs 14:30

When you are jealous and quarrel among yourselves, aren't you influenced by your corrupt nature and living by human standards?

1 Corinthians 3:3b

Love is patient. Love is kind. Love isn't jealous. It doesn't sing its own praises. It isn't arrogant.

1 Corinthians 13:4

 KINDNESS

A person's anxiety will weigh him down,
    but an encouraging word makes him joyful.

Proverbs 12:25

But the spiritual nature produces love, joy, peace, patience, kindness, goodness, faithfulness.

Galatians 5:22

Be kind to each other, sympathetic, forgiving each other as God has forgiven you through Christ.

Ephesians 4:32

Make sure that no one ever pays back one wrong with another wrong. Instead, always try to do what is good for each other and everyone else.

1 Thessalonians 5:15

⚮ KINDNESS OF GOD ⚮

"I hid my face from you for a moment in a burst of anger,
  but I will have compassion on you with everlasting kindness,"
    says the LORD your defender.

Isaiah 54:8

I will acknowledge the LORD's acts of mercy,
  and ⌊sing⌋ the praises of the LORD,
    because of everything that the LORD has done for us.
      He has done many good things for the nation of Israel
        because of his compassion and his unlimited mercy.

Isaiah 63:7

Rather, love your enemies, help them, and lend to them without expecting to get anything back. Then you will have a great reward. You will be the children of the Most High God. After all, he is kind to unthankful and evil people.

Luke 6:35

Do you have contempt for God, who is very kind to you, puts up with you, and deals patiently with you? Don't you realize that it is God's kindness that is trying to lead you to him and change the way you think and act?

Romans 2:4

God has brought us back to life together with Christ Jesus and has given us a position in heaven with him. He did this through Christ Jesus out of his generosity to us in order to show his extremely rich kindness in the world to come.

Ephesians 2:6-7

However, when God our Savior made his kindness and love for humanity appear, he saved us, but not because of anything we had done to gain his approval. Instead, because of his mercy he saved us through the washing in which the Holy Spirit gives us new birth and renewal.

Titus 3:4-5

✎ LONELINESS ✎

God places lonely people in families.
   He leads prisoners out of prison into productive lives,
      but rebellious people must live in an unproductive land.

Psalm 68:6

Yet, I am always with you.
   You hold on to my right hand.

Psalm 73:23

Jesus said . . . "And remember that I am always with you until the end of time."

Matthew 28:20b

I will not leave you all alone. I will come back to you.

John 14:18

∽ **LONGINGS** ∽

The LORD is my shepherd.
    I am never in need.

Psalm 23:1

You know all my desires, O Lord,
    and my groaning has not been hidden from you.

Psalm 38:9

As a deer longs for flowing streams,
    so my soul longs for you, O God.

Psalm 42:1

My soul longs and yearns
    for the LORD'S courtyards.
My whole body shouts for joy to the living God.

Psalm 84:2

❧ LOVE OF GOD ❧

The LORD appeared to me in a faraway place and said,
"I love you with an everlasting love.
So I will continue to show you my kindness."

Jeremiah 31:3

God loved the world this way: He gave his only Son so that everyone who believes in him will not die but will have eternal life.

John 3:16

Christ died for us while we were still sinners. This demonstrates God's love for us.

Romans 5:8

God has shown us his love by sending his only Son into the world so that we could have life through him.

1 John 4:9

We have known and believed that God loves us. God is love. Those who live in God's love live in God, and God lives in them.

1 John 4:16

⁓ **MERCY** ⁓

The LORD your God is a merciful God. He will not abandon you, destroy you, or forget the promise to your ancestors that he swore he would keep.

Deuteronomy 4:31

He has not treated us as we deserve for our sins
   or paid us back for our wrongs.

Psalm 103:10

But from everlasting to everlasting,
   the LORD's mercy is on those who fear him.
     His righteousness belongs
      to their children and grandchildren.

Psalm 103:17

Blessed are those who show mercy.
   They will be treated mercifully.

Matthew 5:7

Be merciful as your Father is merciful.

Luke 6:36

❧ MISTAKES ❧

Do not remember the sins of my youth or my rebellious ways.
Remember me, O Lord, in keeping with your mercy
and your goodness.

Psalm 25:7

Blessed is the person whose disobedience is forgiven
and whose sin is pardoned.
Blessed is the person whom the Lord never accuses of sin
and who has no deceitful thoughts.

Psalm 32:1-2

I made my sins known to you, and I did not cover up my guilt.
I decided to confess them to you, O Lord.
Then you forgave all my sins.

Psalm 32:5

As far as the east is from the west—
that is how far he has removed our rebellious acts from himself.

Psalm 103:12

Whoever covers over his sins does not prosper.
Whoever confesses and abandons them receives compassion.

Proverbs 28:13

We know that all things work together for the good of those who love God—those whom he has called according to his plan.

Romans 8:28

❧ MONEY ❧

No one can serve two masters. He will hate the first master and love the second, or he will be devoted to the first and despise the second. You cannot serve God and wealth.

Matthew 6:24

He told the people, "Be careful to guard yourselves from every kind of greed. Life is not about having a lot of material possessions."

Luke 12:15

We didn't bring anything into the world, and we can't take anything out of it. As long as we have food and clothes, we should be satisfied.

But people who want to get rich keep falling into temptation. They are trapped by many stupid and harmful desires which drown them in destruction and ruin. Certainly, the love of money is the root of all kinds of evil. Some people who have set their hearts on getting rich have wandered away from the Christian faith and have caused themselves a lot of grief.

1 Timothy 6:7-10

Don't love money. Be happy with what you have because God has said, "I will never abandon you or leave you."

Hebrews 13:5

MOURNING

The LORD is near to those whose hearts are humble.
He saves those whose spirits are crushed.

Psalm 34:18

Morning, noon, and night I complain and groan,
 and he listens to my voice.

Psalm 55:17

Blessed are those who mourn.
 They will be comforted.

Matthew 5:4

Come to me, all who are tired from carrying heavy loads, and I will give you rest.

Matthew 11:28

I'm leaving you peace. I'm giving you my peace. I don't give you the kind of peace that the world gives. So don't be troubled or cowardly.

John 14:27

We know that all things work together for the good of those who love God—those whom he has called according to his plan.

Romans 8:28

He will wipe every tear from their eyes. There won't be any more death. There won't be any grief, crying, or pain, because the first things have disappeared.

Revelation 21:4

∽ **OVERWHELMED** ∽

I look up toward the mountains.
   Where can I find help?
My help comes from the LORD,
   the maker of heaven and earth.

Psalm 121:1-2

When you go through the sea, I am with you.
When you go through rivers, they will not sweep you away.
When you walk through fire, you will not be burned,
   and the flames will not harm you.

Isaiah 43:2

The LORD is good.
⌊He is⌋ a fortress in the day of trouble.
He knows those who seek shelter in him.

Nahum 1:7

In every way we're troubled, but we aren't crushed by our troubles. We're frustrated, but we don't give up. We're persecuted, but we're not abandoned. We're captured, but we're not killed.

2 Corinthians 4:8-9

Never worry about anything. But in every situation let God know what you need in prayers and requests while giving thanks. Then God's peace, which goes beyond anything we can imagine, will guard your thoughts and emotions through Christ Jesus.

Philippians 4:6-7

❧ PAIN ❧

Even though I walk through the dark valley of death,
because you are with me, I fear no harm.
Your rod and your staff give me courage.

Psalm 23:4

He is the healer of the brokenhearted.
He is the one who bandages their wounds.

Psalm 147:3

Blessed are those who mourn.
  They will be comforted.

Matthew 5:4

Come to me, all who are tired from carrying heavy loads, and I will give
you rest.

Matthew 11:28

I am convinced that nothing can ever separate us from God's love which
Christ Jesus our Lord shows us. We can't be separated by death or life, by
angels or rulers, by anything in the present or anything in the future, by
forces or powers in the world above or in the world below, or by anything
else in creation.

Romans 8:38-39

He comforts us whenever we suffer. That is why whenever other people
suffer, we are able to comfort them by using the same comfort we have
received from God.

2 Corinthians 1:4

That is why we are not discouraged. Though outwardly we are wearing out, inwardly we are renewed day by day.

2 Corinthians 4:16

PANIC

Listen, Israel, today you're going into battle against your enemies. Don't lose your courage! Don't be afraid or alarmed or tremble because of them.

Deuteronomy 20:3

I called on the LORD in my distress.
  I cried to my God for help.
    He heard my voice from his temple,
      and my cry for help reached his ears.

Psalm 18:6

The LORD will answer you in times of trouble.
The name of the God of Jacob will protect you.

Psalm 20:1

God is our refuge and strength,
  an ever-present help in times of trouble.
That is why we are not afraid

even when the earth quakes
    or the mountains topple into the depths of the sea.

Psalm 46:1-2

Let go ⌊of your concerns⌋!
    Then you will know that I am God.
        I rule the nations.
        I rule the earth.

Psalm 46:10

Don't be afraid, because I am with you.
Don't be intimidated; I am your God.
    I will strengthen you.
    I will help you.
    I will support you with my victorious right hand.

Isaiah 41:10

I know the plans that I have for you, declares the LORD. They are plans for peace and not disaster, plans to give you a future filled with hope.

Jeremiah 29:11

⤳ PATIENCE ⤳

Surrender yourself to the LORD, and wait patiently for him.
  Do not be preoccupied with ⌊an evildoer⌋ who succeeds in his way
    when he carries out his schemes.

Psalm 37:7

A person with good sense is patient,
  and it is to his credit that he overlooks an offense.

Proverbs 19:11

We encourage you, brothers and sisters, to instruct those who are not
living right, cheer up those who are discouraged, help the weak, and be
patient with everyone.

1 Thessalonians 5:14

However, I was treated with mercy so that Christ Jesus could use me, the
foremost sinner, to demonstrate his patience. This patience serves as an
example for those who would believe in him and live forever.

1 Timothy 1:16

You, too, must be patient. Don't give up hope. The Lord will soon be here.

James 5:8

The Lord isn't slow to do what he promised, as some people think. Rather,
he is patient for your sake. He doesn't want to destroy anyone but wants all

people to have an opportunity to turn to him and change the way they think and act.

2 Peter 3:9

∾ PEACE ∾

The LORD will give power to his people.
The LORD will bless his people with peace.

Psalm 29:11

Let go ⌊of your concerns⌋!
   Then you will know that I am God.
      I rule the nations.
      I rule the earth.

Psalm 46:10

A child will be born for us.
A son will be given to us.
   The government will rest on his shoulders.
   He will be named:
      Wonderful Counselor,
      Mighty God,
      Everlasting Father,
      Prince of Peace.

Isaiah 9:6

Now that we have God's approval because of faith, we have peace with God because of what our Lord Jesus Christ has done.

Romans 5:1

In every way we're troubled, but we aren't crushed by our troubles. We're frustrated, but we don't give up. We're persecuted, but we're not abandoned. We're captured, but we're not killed.

2 Corinthians 4:8-9

Also, let Christ's peace control you. God has called you into this peace by bringing you into one body. Be thankful.

Colossians 3:15

❧ PEER PRESSURE ❧

Blessed is the person who does not
　　follow the advice of wicked people,
　　　　take the path of sinners,
　　　　　　or join the company of mockers.

Psalm 1:1

My son,
　　if sinners lure you, do not go along.

Proverbs 1:10

Don't let anyone deceive you. Associating with bad people will ruin decent people.

1 Corinthians 15:33

Am I saying this now to win the approval of people or God? Am I trying to please people? If I were still trying to please people, I would not be Christ's servant.

Galatians 1:10

∽ **PERSECUTION** ∽

The reason I can ⌊still⌋ find hope is that I keep this one thing in mind:
the LORD's mercy.
    We were not completely wiped out.
    His compassion is never limited.
        It is new every morning.
        His faithfulness is great.

Lamentations 3:21-23

Blessed are those who are persecuted
    for doing what God approves of.
The kingdom of heaven belongs to them.

Matthew 5:10

Those who try to live a godly life because they believe in Christ Jesus will be persecuted.

2 Timothy 3:12

If you are insulted because of the name of Christ, you are blessed because the Spirit of glory—the Spirit of God—is resting on you.

1 Peter 4:14

If you suffer for being a Christian, don't feel ashamed, but praise God for being called that name.

1 Peter 4:16

❧ PERSEVERANCE ❧

We can't allow ourselves to get tired of living the right way. Certainly, each of us will receive ⌊everlasting life⌋ at the proper time, if we don't give up.

Galatians 6:9

May the Lord direct your lives as you show God's love and Christ's endurance.

2 Thessalonians 3:5

Brothers and sisters, we can't allow ourselves to get tired of doing what is right.

2 Thessalonians 3:13

I have fought the good fight. I have completed the race. I have kept the faith.

2 Timothy 4:7

∞ **POWER** ∞

The LORD is my light and my salvation.
  Who is there to fear?
The LORD is my life's fortress.
  Who is there to be afraid of?

Psalm 27:1

Our Lord is great, and his power is great.
There is no limit to his understanding.

Psalm 147:5

Praise him for his mighty acts.
Praise him for his immense greatness.

Psalm 150:2

You won't ⌊succeed⌋ by might or by power, but by my Spirit, says the LORD of Armies.

Zechariah 4:6b

But you will receive power when the Holy Spirit comes to you. Then you will be my witnesses to testify about me in Jerusalem, throughout Judea and Samaria, and to the ends of the earth.

Acts 1:8

I'm not ashamed of the Good News. It is God's power to save everyone who believes, Jews first and Greeks as well.

Romans 1:16

God's kingdom is not just talk, it is power.

1 Corinthians 4:20

PRAYER

Call on me in times of trouble.
 I will rescue you, and you will honor me.

Psalm 50:15

Before they call, I will answer.
While they're still speaking, I will hear.

Isaiah 65:24

When you pray, go to your room and close the door. Pray privately to your Father who is with you. Your Father sees what you do in private. He will reward you.

Matthew 6:6

Ask, and you will receive. Search, and you will find. Knock, and the door will be opened for you. Everyone who asks will receive. The one who searches will find, and for the one who knocks, the door will be opened.

Matthew 7:7-8

Pray in the Spirit in every situation. Use every kind of prayer and request there is. For the same reason be alert. Use every kind of effort and make every kind of request for all of God's people.

Ephesians 6:18

Never stop praying.

1 Thessalonians 5:17

❧ **PRESSURE** ❧

I went to the LORD for help.
    He answered me and rescued me from all my fears.

Psalm 34:4

Turn your burdens over to the LORD,
    and he will take care of you.
        He will never let the righteous person stumble.

Psalm 55:22

Thanks be to the Lord,
  who daily carries our burdens for us.
    God is our salvation.

Psalm 68:19

Don't be afraid, because I am with you.
Don't be intimidated; I am your God.
  I will strengthen you.
  I will help you.
  I will support you with my victorious right hand.

Isaiah 41:10

We were not completely wiped out.
His compassion is never limited.
  It is new every morning.
  His faithfulness is great.

Lamentations 3:22-23

In every way we're troubled, but we aren't crushed by our troubles. We're frustrated, but we don't give up.

2 Corinthians 4:8

⋙ **PROBLEMS** ⋘

God is our refuge and strength,
    an ever-present help in times of trouble.

Psalm 46:1

When I am in trouble, I call out to you
    because you answer me.

Psalm 86:7

I look up toward the mountains.
    Where can I find help?
My help comes from the LORD,
    the maker of heaven and earth.

Psalm 121:1-2

Even though I walk into the middle of trouble,
    you guard my life against the anger of my enemies.
    You stretch out your hand,
        and your right hand saves me.

Psalm 138:7

If any of you are having trouble, pray. If you are happy, sing psalms.

James 5:13

❧ **PURITY** ❧

Create a clean heart in me, O God,
  and renew a faithful spirit within me.

Psalm 51:10

Blessed are those whose thoughts are pure.
  They will see God.

Matthew 5:8

Finally, brothers and sisters, keep your thoughts on whatever is right or deserves praise: things that are true, honorable, fair, pure, acceptable, or commendable.

Philippians 4:8

But if we live in the light in the same way that God is in the light, we have a relationship with each other. And the blood of his Son Jesus cleanses us from every sin.

1 John 1:7

Nothing unclean, no one who does anything detestable, and no liars will ever enter it. Only those whose names are written in the lamb's Book of Life will enter it.

Revelation 21:27

❧ **RELIEF** ❧

He reached down from high above and took hold of me.
He pulled me out of the raging water.

Psalm 18:16

In their distress they cried out to the LORD.
   He rescued them from their troubles.

Psalm 107:6

You saved me from death.
You saved my eyes from tears ⌊and⌋ my feet from stumbling.

Psalm 116:8

Come to me, all who are tired from carrying heavy loads, and I will give
you rest.

Matthew 11:28

He will wipe every tear from their eyes. There won't be any more death.
There won't be any grief, crying, or pain, because the first things have
disappeared.

Revelation 21:4

❧ REST ❧

I fall asleep in peace the moment I lie down
    because you alone, O LORD, enable me to live securely.

Psalm 4:8

He renews my soul.
He guides me along the paths of righteousness
    for the sake of his name.

Psalm 23:3

I waited patiently for the LORD.
    He turned to me and heard my cry for help.
    He pulled me out of a horrible pit,
        out of the mud and clay.
    He set my feet on a rock
        and made my steps secure.
    He placed a new song in my mouth,
        a song of praise to our God.
            Many will see this and worship.
            They will trust the LORD.

Psalm 40:1-3

Wait calmly for God alone, my soul,
    because my hope comes from him.

Psalm 62:5

Come to me, all who are tired from carrying heavy loads, and I will give you rest.

Matthew 11:28

꩜ **RISK-TAKING** ꩜

I have commanded you, "Be strong and courageous! Don't tremble or be terrified, because the LORD your God is with you wherever you go."

Joshua 1:9

Those who want to save their lives will lose them. But those who lose their lives for me will find them.

Matthew 16:25

But he told me: "My kindness is all you need. My power is strongest when you are weak." So I will brag even more about my weaknesses in order that Christ's power will live in me.

2 Corinthians 12:9

It's far more than that! I consider everything else worthless because I'm much better off knowing Christ Jesus my Lord. It's because of him that I think of everything as worthless. I threw it all away in order to gain Christ

Philippians 3:8

So we can confidently say,
   "The Lord is my helper.
     I will not be afraid.
       What can mortals do to me?"

Hebrews 13:6

SADNESS

You have seen ⌊it⌋; yes, you have taken note of trouble and grief
   and placed them under your control.
     The victim entrusts himself to you.
You alone have been the helper of orphans.

Psalm 10:14

O LORD, you light my lamp.
   My God turns my darkness into light.

Psalm 18:28

Even though I walk through the dark valley of death,
  because you are with me, I fear no harm.
    Your rod and your staff give me courage.

Psalm 23:4

The LORD is near to those whose hearts are humble.
He saves those whose spirits are crushed.

Psalm 34:18

He is the healer of the brokenhearted.
He is the one who bandages their wounds.

Psalm 147:3

He will wipe every tear from their eyes. There won't be any more death.
There won't be any grief, crying, or pain, because the first things have
disappeared.

Revelation 21:4

⤳ SAFETY ⤳

But you, O LORD, are a shield that surrounds me.
  You are my glory.
  You hold my head high.

Psalm 3:3

The LORD is my rock and my fortress and my Savior,
　my God, my rock in whom I take refuge,
　　my shield, and the strength of my salvation,
　　　my stronghold.

Psalm 18:2

He hides me in his shelter when there is trouble.
He keeps me hidden in his tent.
He sets me high on a rock.

Psalm 27:5

He will put his angels in charge of you
　to protect you in all your ways.

Psalm 91:11

During times of trouble I called on the LORD.
　The LORD answered me ⌊and⌋ set me free ⌊from all of them⌋.
The LORD is on my side.
　I am not afraid.
　　What can mortals do to me?

Psalm 118:5-6

O LORD, you have examined me, and you know me.
　You alone know when I sit down and when I get up.
　You read my thoughts from far away. . . .

You are all around me—in front of me and in back of me.
You lay your hand on me.

Psalm 139:1-2, 5

Aren't five sparrows sold for two cents? God doesn't forget any of them.
Even every hair on your head has been counted. Don't be afraid! You are
worth more than many sparrows.

Luke 12:6-7

∽ SATISFACTION ∽

Naked I came from my mother,
　　and naked I will return.
The LORD has given,
　　and the LORD has taken away!
May the name of the LORD be praised.

Job 1:21

Whoever loves money will never be satisfied with money. Whoever loves
wealth will never be satisfied with more income. Even this is pointless.

Ecclesiastes 5:10

I'm not saying this because I'm in any need. I've learned to be content in whatever situation I'm in. I know how to live in poverty or prosperity. No matter what the situation, I've learned the secret of how to live when I'm full or when I'm hungry, when I have too much or when I have too little.

Philippians 4:11-12

A godly life brings huge profits to people who are content with what they have.

1 Timothy 6:6

✥ SECOND COMING ✥ OF CHRIST

The Son of Man will come with his angels in his Father's glory. Then he will pay back each person based on what that person has done.

Matthew 16:27

This Good News about the kingdom will be spread throughout the world as a testimony to all nations. Then the end will come.

Matthew 24:14

My Father's house has many rooms. If that were not true, would I have told you that I'm going to prepare a place for you? If I go to prepare a place for you, I will come again. Then I will bring you into my presence so that you will be where I am.

John 14:2-3

I'm telling you a mystery. Not all of us will die, but we will all be changed. It will happen in an instant, in a split second at the sound of the last trumpet. Indeed, that trumpet will sound, and then the dead will come back to life. They will be changed so that they can live forever.

1 Corinthians 15:51-52

The Lord will come from heaven with a command, with the voice of the archangel, and with the trumpet ⌊call⌋ of God. First, the dead who believed in Christ will come back to life. Then, together with them, we who are still alive will be taken in the clouds to meet the Lord in the air. In this way we will always be with the Lord.

1 Thessalonians 4:16-17

The day of the Lord will come like a thief. On that day heaven will pass away with a roaring sound. Everything that makes up the universe will burn and be destroyed. The earth and everything that people have done on it will be exposed.

2 Peter 3:10

✺ SECURITY ✺

The eternal God is your shelter,
　　and his everlasting arms support you.
He will force your enemies out of your way
　　and tell you to destroy them.

Deuteronomy 33:27

The LORD is my rock and my fortress and my Savior,
　　my God, my rock in whom I take refuge,
　　　　my shield, and the strength of my salvation,
　　　　　　my stronghold.

Psalm 18:2

Even though an army sets up camp against me,
　　my heart will not be afraid.
Even though a war breaks out against me,
　　I will still have confidence ⌊in the LORD⌋.

Psalm 27:3

You are my hiding place.
You protect me from trouble.
You surround me with joyous songs of salvation.

Psalm 32:7

The name of the LORD is a strong tower.
    A righteous person runs to it and is safe.

Proverbs 18:10

I give them eternal life. They will never be lost, and no one will tear them away from me.

John 10:28

∾ SELFISHNESS ∾

Then Jesus said to his disciples, "Those who want to come with me must say no to the things they want, pick up their crosses, and follow me."

Matthew 16:24

Whoever wants to be the most important person must take the last place and be a servant to everyone else.

Mark 9:35b

He told the people, "Be careful to guard yourselves from every kind of greed. Life is not about having a lot of material possessions."

Luke 12:15

People should be concerned about others and not just about themselves.

1 Corinthians 10:24

Don't act out of selfish ambition or be conceited. Instead, humbly think of others as being better than yourselves.

Philippians 2:3

 **SERVICE**

Who's the greatest, the person who sits at the table or the servant? Isn't it really the person who sits at the table? But I'm among you as a servant.

Luke 22:27

Serve eagerly as if you were serving your heavenly master and not merely serving human masters.

Ephesians 6:7

[Jesus Christ] emptied himself by taking on the form of a servant,
   by becoming like other humans,
   by having a human appearance.

Philippians 2:7

Whatever you do, do it wholeheartedly as though you were working for your real master and not merely for humans. You know that your real master will give you an inheritance as your reward. It is Christ, your real master, whom you are serving.

Colossians 3:23-24

∾ **SHAME** ∾

I trust you, O my God.
    Do not let me be put to shame.
    Do not let my enemies triumph over me.
No one who waits for you will ever be put to shame,
    but all who are unfaithful will be put to shame.

Psalm 25:2-3

I made my sins known to you, and I did not cover up my guilt.
I decided to confess them to you, O LORD.
    Then you forgave all my sins.

Psalm 32:5

All who look to him will be radiant.
    Their faces will never be covered with shame.

Psalm 34:5

The LORD is near to those whose hearts are humble.
He saves those whose spirits are crushed.

Psalm 34:18

Wash me thoroughly from my guilt,
    and cleanse me from my sin.

Purify me from sin with hyssop, and I will be clean.
Wash me, and I will be whiter than snow.

Psalm 51:2, 7

I'm not ashamed of the Good News. It is God's power to save everyone who believes, Jews first and Greeks as well.

Romans 1:16

Scripture says, "Whoever believes in him will not be ashamed."

Romans 10:11

Do your best to present yourself to God as a tried-and-true worker who isn't ashamed to teach the word of truth correctly.

2 Timothy 2:15

⊱ SICKNESS ⊰

Be strong, all who wait with hope for the LORD,
    and let your heart be courageous.

Psalm 31:24

The LORD will support him on his sickbed.
    You will restore this person to health when he is ill.

Psalm 41:3

Praise the LORD, my soul,
and never forget all the good he has done:
He is the one who forgives all your sins,
the one who heals all your diseases.

Psalm 103:2-3

He sent his message and healed them.
He rescued them from the grave.

Psalm 107:20

A joyful heart is good medicine,
but depression drains one's strength.

Proverbs 17:22

Praise the God and Father of our Lord Jesus Christ! He is the Father who is compassionate and the God who gives comfort. He comforts us whenever we suffer. That is why whenever other people suffer, we are able to comfort them by using the same comfort we have received from God.

2 Corinthians 1:3-4

Prayers offered in faith will save those who are sick, and the Lord will cure them.

James 5:15a

❧ SORROW ❧

You have changed my sobbing into dancing.
You have removed my sackcloth and clothed me with joy

Psalm 30:11

I will rejoice and be glad because of your mercy.
   You have seen my misery.
   You have known the troubles in my soul.

Psalm 31:7

The LORD is near to those whose hearts are humble.
He saves those whose spirits are crushed.

Psalm 34:18

❧ SPIRITUAL GROWTH ❧

Brothers and sisters, because of God's compassion toward us, I encourage
you to offer your bodies as living sacrifices, dedicated to God and pleasing
to him. This kind of worship is appropriate for you. Don't become like the
people of this world. Instead, change the way you think. Then you will
always be able to determine what God really wants—what is good,
pleasing, and perfect.

Romans 12:1-2

I'm convinced that God, who began this good work in you, will carry it through to completion on the day of Christ Jesus.

Philippians 1:6

We ask this so that you will live the kind of lives that prove you belong to the Lord. Then you will want to please him in every way as you grow in producing every kind of good work by this knowledge about God.

Colossians 1:10

Stay away from lusts which tempt young people. Pursue what has God's approval. Pursue faith, love, and peace together with those who worship the Lord with a pure heart.

2 Timothy 2:22

Desire God's pure word as newborn babies desire milk. Then you will grow in your salvation.

1 Peter 2:2

Because of this, make every effort to add integrity to your faith; and to integrity add knowledge; to knowledge add self-control; to self-control add endurance; to endurance add godliness.

2 Peter 1:5-6

But grow in the good will and knowledge of our Lord and Savior Jesus Christ. Glory belongs to him now and for that eternal day! Amen.

2 Peter 3:18

❧ STRENGTH ❧

Love the LORD your God with all your heart, with all your soul, and with all your strength.

Deuteronomy 6:5

The LORD's eyes scan the whole world to find those whose hearts are committed to him and to strengthen them.

2 Chronicles 16:9a

Yet, the strength of those who wait with hope in the LORD
   will be renewed.
      They will soar on wings like eagles.
         They will run and won't become weary.

Isaiah 40:31

They will walk and won't grow tired.
Don't be afraid, because I am with you.
Don't be intimidated; I am your God.
   I will strengthen you.
   I will help you.
   I will support you with my victorious right hand.

Isaiah 41:10

I can do everything through Christ who strengthens me.

Philippians 4:13

❧ **STRESS** ❧

I called on the LORD in my distress.
I cried to my God for help.
He heard my voice from his temple,
and my cry for help reached his ears.

Psalm 18:6

Have pity on me, O LORD, because I am in distress.
My eyes, my soul, and my body waste away from grief.

Psalm 31:9

Thanks be to the Lord,
who daily carries our burdens for us.
God is our salvation.

Psalm 68:19

When you go through the sea, I am with you.
When you go through rivers, they will not sweep you away.
When you walk through fire, you will not be burned,
and the flames will not harm you.

Isaiah 43:2

Come to me, all who are tired from carrying heavy loads, and I will give you rest.

Matthew 11:28

Never worry about anything. But in every situation let God know what you need in prayers and requests while giving thanks. Then God's peace, which goes beyond anything we can imagine, will guard your thoughts and emotions through Christ Jesus.

Philippians 4:6-7

STRIFE

Whoever forgives an offense seeks love,
    but whoever keeps bringing up the issue
        separates the closest of friends.

Proverbs 17:9

Avoiding a quarrel is honorable.
    After all, any stubborn fool can start a fight.

Proverbs 20:3

Stop judging, and you will never be judged. Stop condemning, and you will never be condemned. Forgive, and you will be forgiven.

Luke 6:37

When you are jealous and quarrel among yourselves, aren't you influenced by your corrupt nature and living by human standards?

1 Corinthians 3:3b

Put up with each other, and forgive each other if anyone has a complaint. Forgive as the Lord forgave you.

Colossians 3:13

❦ STRUGGLES ❦

The LORD is fighting for you! So be still!

Exodus 14:14

This is not a wrestling match against a human opponent. We are wrestling with rulers, authorities, the powers who govern this world of darkness, and spiritual forces that control evil in the heavenly world.

Ephesians 6:12

I work hard and struggle to do this while his mighty power works in me.

Colossians 1:29

Fight the good fight for the Christian faith. Take hold of everlasting life to which you were called and about which you made a good testimony in front of many witnesses.

1 Timothy 6:12

You struggle against sin, but your struggles haven't killed you.

Hebrews 12:4

✎ **SUCCESS** ✎

Only be strong and very courageous, faithfully doing everything in the teachings that my servant Moses commanded you. Don't turn away from them. Then you will succeed wherever you go.

Joshua 1:7

Without advice plans go wrong,
but with many advisers they succeed.

Proverbs 15:22

Entrust your efforts to the LORD,
and your plans will succeed.

Proverbs 16:3

✎ **SUFFERING** ✎

You have heard the desire of oppressed people, O LORD.
You encourage them.
You pay close attention to them

Psalm 10:17

The LORD has not despised or been disgusted
   with the plight of the oppressed one.
      He has not hidden his face from that person.
         The LORD heard when that oppressed person
            cried out to him for help.

Psalm 22:24

But that's not all. We also brag when we are suffering. We know that
suffering creates endurance, endurance creates character, and character
creates confidence.

Romans 5:3

I consider our present sufferings insignificant compared to the glory that
will soon be revealed to us.

Romans 8:18

God has given you the privilege not only to believe in Christ but also to
suffer for him.

Philippians 1:29

Turn all your anxiety over to God because he cares for you.

1 Peter 5:7

❧ TEMPTATION ❧

There isn't any temptation that you have experienced which is unusual for humans. God, who faithfully keeps his promises, will not allow you to be tempted beyond your power to resist. But when you are tempted, he will also give you the ability to endure the temptation as your way of escape.

1 Corinthians 10:13

For this reason, take up all the armor that God supplies. Then you will be able to take a stand during these evil days. Once you have overcome all obstacles, you will be able to stand your ground.

Ephesians 6:13

After all, God's saving kindness has appeared for the benefit of all people. It trains us to avoid ungodly lives filled with worldly desires so that we can live self-controlled, moral, and godly lives in this present world.

Titus 2:11-12

Because Jesus experienced temptation when he suffered, he is able to help others when they are tempted.

Hebrews 2:18

So place yourselves under God's authority. Resist the devil, and he will run away from you.

James 4:7

❧ THANKFULNESS ❧

I will give thanks to the LORD for his righteousness.
I will make music to praise the name of the LORD Most High.

Psalm 7:17

Enter his gates with a song of thanksgiving.
Come into his courtyards with a song of praise.
Give thanks to him; praise his name.

Psalm 100:4

Give thanks to the LORD because he is good,
    because his mercy endures forever.

Psalm 107:1

Never worry about anything. But in every situation let God know what you
need in prayers and requests while giving thanks.

Philippians 4:6

Whatever happens, give thanks, because it is God's will in Christ Jesus that
you do this.

1 Thessalonians 5:18

❧ TRIALS ❧

The victory for righteous people comes from the LORD.
  He is their fortress in times of trouble.

Psalm 37:39

Because Christ suffered so much for us, we can receive so much comfort
from him.

2 Corinthians 1:5

Our suffering is light and temporary and is producing for us an eternal
glory that is greater than anything we can imagine.

2 Corinthians 4:17

Dear friends, don't be surprised by the fiery troubles that are coming in
order to test you. Don't feel as though something strange is happening to
you.

1 Peter 4:12

Since the Lord did all this, he knows how to rescue godly people when they
are tested. He also knows how to hold immoral people for punishment on
the day of judgment.

2 Peter 2:9

≈ **TROUBLES** ≈

Even though I walk through the dark valley of death,
    because you are with me, I fear no harm.
        Your rod and your staff give me courage.

Psalm 23:4

Relieve my troubled heart,
    and bring me out of my distress.

Psalm 25:17

Why are you discouraged, my soul?
Why are you so restless?
    Put your hope in God,
        because I will still praise him.
            He is my savior and my God.

Psalm 42:5

Turn your burdens over to the LORD,
    and he will take care of you.
        He will never let the righteous person stumble.

Psalm 55:22

The LORD is good.
⌊He is⌋ a fortress in the day of trouble.
He knows those who seek shelter in him.

Nahum 1:7

Come to me, all who are tired from carrying heavy loads, and I will give
you rest.

Matthew 11:28

Praise the God and Father of our Lord Jesus Christ! He is the Father who
is compassionate and the God who gives comfort. He comforts us
whenever we suffer. That is why whenever other people suffer, we are able
to comfort them by using the same comfort we have received from God.

2 Corinthians 1:3-4

❦ UNFAIRNESS ❦

"Because oppressed people are robbed and needy people groan,
I will now arise," says the LORD.
"I will provide safety for those who long for it."

Psalm 12:5

This is what happens to everyone
   who is greedy for unjust gain.
      Greed takes away his life.

Proverbs 1:19

Dishonest scales are disgusting to the LORD,
   but accurate weights are pleasing to him.

Proverbs 11:1

Bless those who curse you. Pray for those who insult you.

Luke 6:28

❧ **VICTORY** ❧

Only be strong and very courageous, faithfully doing everything in the teachings that my servant Moses commanded you. Don't turn away from them. Then you will succeed wherever you go.

Joshua 1:7

Blessed is the person who does not
   follow the advice of wicked people,
      take the path of sinners,
         or join the company of mockers.
Rather, he delights in the teachings of the LORD
   and reflects on his teachings day and night.

He is like a tree planted beside streams—
   a tree that produces fruit in season
      and whose leaves do not wither.
He succeeds in everything he does.

Psalm 1:1-3

The one who loves us gives us an overwhelming victory in all these difficulties.

Romans 8:37

When this body that decays is changed into a body that cannot decay, and this mortal body is changed into a body that will live forever, then the teaching of Scripture will come true:
   "Death is turned into victory!"

1 Corinthians 15:54

Thank God that he gives us the victory through our Lord Jesus Christ.

1 Corinthians 15:57

Everyone who has been born from God has won the victory over the world. Our faith is what wins the victory over the world. Who wins the victory over the world? Isn't it the person who believes that Jesus is the Son of God?

1 John 5:4-5

∽ **VULNERABILITY** ∽

You have seen ⌊it⌋; yes, you have taken note of trouble and grief
   and placed them under your control.
     The victim entrusts himself to you.
You alone have been the helper of orphans.

Psalm 10:14

"Because oppressed people are robbed and needy people groan,
   I will now arise," says the LORD.
   "I will provide safety for those who long for it."

Psalm 12:5

You have been my refuge,
   a tower of strength against the enemy.

Psalm 61:3

They will not come near you,
   even though a thousand may fall dead beside you
     or ten thousand at your right side.

Psalm 91:7

When you go through the sea, I am with you.
When you go through rivers, they will not sweep you away.

When you walk through fire, you will not be burned,
   and the flames will not harm you.

Isaiah 43:2

 WEAKNESS

The LORD is my light and my salvation.
   Who is there to fear?
The LORD is my life's fortress.
   Who is there to be afraid of?

Psalm 27:1

Blessed is the one who has concern for helpless people.
   The LORD will rescue him in times of trouble.

Psalm 41:1

He will have pity on the poor and needy
   and will save the lives of the needy.

Psalm 72:13

When I called, you answered me.
   You made me bold by strengthening my soul.

Psalm 138:3

At the same time the Spirit also helps us in our weakness, because we don't know how to pray for what we need. But the Spirit intercedes along with our groans that cannot be expressed in words.

Romans 8:26

But he told me: "My kindness is all you need. My power is strongest when you are weak." So I will brag even more about my weaknesses in order that Christ's power will live in me. Therefore, I accept weakness, mistreatment, hardship, persecution, and difficulties suffered for Christ. It's clear that when I'm weak, I'm strong.

2 Corinthians 12:9-10

We have a chief priest who is able to sympathize with our weaknesses. He was tempted in every way that we are, but he didn't sin.

Hebrews 4:15

❧ WISDOM ❧

The teachings of the LORD are perfect.
　They renew the soul.
The testimony of the LORD is dependable.
　It makes gullible people wise.

Psalm 19:7

Yet, you desire truth and sincerity.
  Deep down inside me you teach me wisdom.

Psalm 51:6

The fear of the LORD is the beginning of wisdom.
Good sense is shown by everyone
    who follows ⌊God's guiding principles⌋.
His praise continues forever.

Psalm 111:10

I pray that the glorious Father, the God of our Lord Jesus Christ, would
give you a spirit of wisdom and revelation as you come to know Christ
better.

Ephesians 1:17

God has hidden all the treasures of wisdom and knowledge in Christ.

Colossians 2:3

From infancy you have known the Holy Scriptures. They have the power to
give you wisdom so that you can be saved through faith in Christ Jesus.

2 Timothy 3:15

If any of you needs wisdom to know what you should do, you should ask
God, and he will give it to you. God is generous to everyone and doesn't
find fault with them.

James 1:5

❧ WORRY ❧

Turn your burdens over to the LORD,
   and he will take care of you.
      He will never let the righteous person stumble.

Psalm 55:22

Thanks be to the Lord,
   who daily carries our burdens for us.
      God is our salvation.

Psalm 68:19

When I worried about many things,
   your assuring words soothed my soul.

Psalm 94:19

So don't ever worry about tomorrow. After all, tomorrow will worry about itself. Each day has enough trouble of its own.

Matthew 6:34

My God will richly fill your every need in a glorious way through Christ Jesus.

Philippians 4:19

Also, let Christ's peace control you. God has called you into this peace by
bringing you into one body. Be thankful.

Colossians 3:15

✎ WRONGS ✎

Do not remember the sins of my youth or my rebellious ways.
   Remember me, O LORD, in keeping with your mercy
      and your goodness.

Psalm 25:7

Blessed is the person whose disobedience is forgiven
   and whose sin is pardoned.
Blessed is the person whom the LORD never accuses of sin
   and who has no deceitful thoughts.

Psalm 32:1-2

I have sinned against you, especially you.
I have done what you consider evil.
   So you hand down justice when you speak,
      and you are blameless when you judge.

Psalm 51:4

SAVE $2

off suggested retail of any GOD'S WORD full-Bible product.

Today's Bible translation that says what it means!

- *GOD'S WORD*, Premier Edition
- *GOD'S WORD* for Each Day
- *GOD'S WORD* Worship Bible
- *GOD'S WORD* Angel Bible

- *GOD'S WORD* for Students
- *GOD'S WORD* for Boys
- *GOD'S WORD* for Girls
- *GOD'S WORD* Large Print

Offer valid at participating bookstores only. Limited to one coupon per purchase. Coupon expires 8/31/97.

To Retailer: World Publishing will credit your account for the wholesale value of each coupon returned. Attach the coupons to a summary sheet listing the number of coupons redeemed, store name, manager name, address, telephone and account number. Savings at publishers suggested retail price. Coupons must be redeemed by 9/15/97. Return coupons to: World Bible Publishers, *GOD'S WORD* Coupon Redemption, P.O. Box 230411, Grand Rapids, MI 49523.

At your local bookstore, or call
1-800-GOD'S-WORD
for the location nearest you.